# *Glory, Hallelujah!*
# *Now Please Pick Up Your Socks*

### Meditations by Jane Ellen Mauldin

Skinner House Books
Boston

Published by Skinner House Books, an imprint of the Unitarian
Universalist Association, 25 Beacon Street, Boston, MA 02108-2800.

Printed in the USA.

ISBN 1-55896-365-0

10 9 8 7 6 5 4 3 2 1
02 01 00 99 98

Library of Congress Cataloging-in-Publication Data

Mauldin, Jane Ellen.
    Glory, hallelujah! : now please pick up your socks : meditations /
by Jane Ellen Mauldin.
        p.   cm.
    ISBN 1-55896-365-0 (alk. paper)
    1. Spiritual life—Unitarian Universalist churches—Meditations.
2. Meditations. I. Title.
BX9855.M38     1998
248.4'89134—dc21                                         98-16742
                                                              CIP

# Contents

# The Holey Robe

Graduation day from seminary was a big event. My mother flew in from another state to cheer me on. Together we remembered the many sacrifices we both had made to get me that far, and we laughed and cried together through the morning. As the time for the ceremony drew near, my mother proudly unpacked my doctoral robe from the factory packing box and volunteered to iron out the many wrinkles. She borrowed an ironing board and a small student travel iron from a seminary housemate, setting them up in the community dining room as I went to prepare myself.

Suddenly I heard a scream of terror and my mother came running down the hall, sobbing, clutching the robe. "I'm so, so sorry, Jane!! I've ruined it! I've ruined it! I couldn't find my reading glasses and I ironed it with the heat too high!" Sure enough, the first doctoral robe ever to be worn by a member of our family had a notable hole, clearly the shape of a travel iron, in the underside of a voluminous sleeve. We hugged and together bemoaned the fate of the robe. There wasn't much to do at the moment. The ceremony would begin in minutes in the church across the street. We wiped our eyes, grabbed our things, and ran.

As I dashed into the church foyer and found my place in a procession just about to begin, my colleagues bent over me in grave concern.

"Where were you?"

"Are you okay?"

I showed them the branded sleeve.

"Oh, that's too bad," said one classmate.

"It will cost a lot to get that sleeve replaced," remarked another, "probably over $100" (an impossible sum for a new seminary graduate).

Then I heard the voice of my friend Patricia, "Why, I think that's dear! Every time you wear your robe, you'll have the memory of your mother with you."

She was right. I have grown to love that sweet hole in my robe. Through it I am connected to my mother and my family. With it I carry all the strength and the pain that I have felt in my family. It reminds me that most of us are "walking wounded," and although the wounds don't always show, they help make us who we are, and help prepare us for the joys and trials of life.

We've begun a new ritual around our dinner table in which each member of the family takes a minute or two to name what he or she is grateful for. No matter how yucky our day has been, we try to offer our gratitude in a spirit of kindness and real thankfulness. Often, the ritual's nicest effect is to calm the troops who may be feeling a bit rowdy or punchy. That's on a good evening. Other times, well . . .

"Today," said I one evening, trying to model appropriate behavior (usually a ludicrous pursuit), "I am thankful for the wonderful rain we had this afternoon, which watered all the trees and grass and flowers so they can grow."

"Today," said Daughter #1, "I am grateful for the rain and the trees and the flowers. And I am grateful for Mom and Dad and Sister and Brother and Dog." (A not-so-subtle attempt at ingratiating herself, as her sly smile implied, but spoken with heartfelt emotion, nonetheless.)

"Today," said Daughter #2, "I am grateful for Mom and Dad and Brother and Dog." A smirk.

"What?" Dad and Mom were stunned. "What about your sister?" Daughter #1 immediately recognized the implications of Daughter #2's statement, which pointedly left her out. She burst into tears and ran from the table.

We continue to work on gratitude circles at our house. Some of us find it hard to be thankful when we would rather be angry. Sometimes even I (who like to consider myself closer to perfect than many) would rather give my husband a swift verbal kick than words of appreciation.

Yet, there is something sacred about our gratitude circles. Gratitude has a healing power at our table that is more tangible than forgiveness or even ice cream. We can't honestly nourish a grudge at the same time that we nourish gratitude.

So we try. Daughter #1 came back to the table and we talked about forgiveness as well as gratitude, and we wondered aloud about pain and healing in words a child might be able to fathom.

And we grown-ups gave a silent sigh of gratitude for yet one more chance to do our job again and go on.

A few days after Hurricane Andrew devastated southern Florida and parts of Louisiana, I heard someone neatly wrapping up the events in Bad Theology. I was listening to my favorite public radio program when a report described a worship service in a Florida church that had been mildly damaged in the hurricane. Volunteers had mended the few holes in the roof with donated plywood, and worship services continued. The minister, however, found deep significance in the lack of major harm done to the building.

"I have driven by Lakeside Baptist Church. It is *gone*!" he roared. "I have driven by Main Street Baptist Church. It is *gone*! I have even driven down to Believers' Baptist Church. It is *gone*! God has spared us!" he concluded. "God has spared *us*!"

How easy it is for some people to examine the conditions of their lives and to conclude that they are better loved by the powers of the universe than a Somalian woman with three children starving in the desert. How easy it is for some people living in comfortable conditions to believe that they deserve all they have and that a man born and raised in inner city slums deserves his lot in life, too.

It would be easy and comfortable to believe these things, but I do not. I am convinced that we are all interconnected. We are all responsible for one another.

5

It is hard to choose my words judiciously after hearing such an adamant declaration of Bad Theology. Yet after the sad and sarcastic responses finished playing through my head, one certainty remains: We who believe otherwise must not keep quiet. To keep our message to ourselves allows such Bad Theology to become the Theology of America.

If a radio reporter ever came to my home, I would say that God is the creative force that has cast each of us into this world. God is the love in and between people. God does not willfully direct hurricanes onto the beaches of the unjust. God is the moral conscience that demands we walk these beaches hand-in-hand, building together where hurricanes have destroyed.

My daughter is not learning to swim. At least, not as fast as I would like her to learn. Liz has been taking swimming lessons for the past two summers and all she can do is paddle a few feet across the pool.

My daughter isn't afraid of the water. She splashes and kicks with abandon, regularly pestering any available parent to swim with her in our backyard pool. You see, Liz doesn't *want* to learn to swim. She isn't ready to take her feet off the bottom of the shallow end and trust her body to the strength of her arms and legs.

The problem for me is that I want Liz to be safe and independent in the pool.

The problem for Liz is quite different: she doesn't want to swim, but she does want to follow her big brother and friends into the deep end, to have full range of the entire pool. An inflatable ring or kickboard is bulky and limits her ability to use her arms to play. There have been no easy answers for Liz.

Until now. I stopped at a yard sale a couple of weeks ago and picked up a child's life jacket in good, but used, condition. Liz claimed it for her own immediately. Now when she enters the pool, she tentatively splashes by herself for a few minutes, then pulls on the jacket and joy streams across her face. She feels free and safe with the life jacket on, and I finally have relented to her request to wear it often.

I want Liz to grow, to become independent and self-reliant. She isn't ready yet. For me, that life jacket represents her need to hang on, if only for a few days or weeks—or even a summer—to her childhood.

Many of us have life jackets: people, beliefs, prayers, or habits that support us through the difficult moments of life. They remind us, when we wear them, that in the Great Swimming Pool of Life, we need the buoyancy provided by a larger spirit, a larger purpose, a larger humanity.

Sometimes, when addiction or destruction is the fabric of our life jackets, we really need to remove them. However, when our life jackets are woven of love, they can be true lifesavers.

There was a time in my life when absolute self-reliance appeared the most honest, dependable route to take. Now I trust myself to my husband's love. I trust myself to the trees outside my window, and the air I breathe, and the god-spirit-holiness-interconnectedness of the universe. I trust that I am not alone, even in my most desolate moments.

I continue to encourage Liz to let go and swim. But only she will know the right time. When she does, I believe she will find that an even greater life jacket—the strength of the universe which runs through her veins—will not let her down. Liz will learn to trust and swim. So, I pray, shall we all.

# *In-Laws*

*For Anne and Richard Lowenburg*

They are an older couple. Not so old in years, yet life has etched its changes on their bodies and circumstances. They have raised and continue to help their now-grown children. They have been loyal and loving to their friends. They have cared for aging parents, giving fully without hesitation or regret.

But now he is ailing. I see them as often as I can, and each time I leave, I am amazed at my own youth and how much I have to learn.

Sometimes I try to visit them with my own agenda: "See here, you should do this, or call that agency, or read this article." I speak authoritatively with all the wisdom that four decades of life have bestowed on me. They listen kindly. They nod, smile, and love me despite my arrogance. Then I depart and they keep on caring for one another in the deep and powerful ways they have for some forty years.

I am humbled before such love. I go home tired to my fussy children and stressed husband and immediately hear words come out of my mouth that have no place in a home of love.

So I take a breath and wonder silently how I might develop the patience and forgiveness that are the corollaries of real love. When will I ever learn?

I watch the man and woman greet each day with gentleness and quiet optimism, despite the looming night. They are my teachers, more surely than any who ever taught me my ABCs.

# *Wakeful Nights*

My wakeful nights are fewer now that my children are growing older. A recent event reminded me of what I am missing. After a tremendously exciting weekend in another state at a family celebration, my young son and I found that our sleep schedules were no longer in sync.

On the way home, Ben slept in the plane and the car and then was awake in his room from 10:00 p.m. until 3:00 a.m. Meanwhile, I was completely, utterly, absolutely exhausted. My husband joined me in physical oblivion because he had just spent the weekend at home, getting up often throughout the nights with a baby daughter who missed her mother. An old back injury was also troubling Harry and he lay drugged, with ice on his back, in great pain.

It was a thousand and one nights that night. Each time I fell asleep, Ben called for me. He was disturbed, afraid, and insecure after his intense weekend of travelling and meeting new people. I grew grumpier and grumpier, padding through a sleeping household to reassure and calm a wakeful child. I felt alone and adrift, aware that I alone could help the child who called out to me, yet desperately needy myself.

I spent the next day with my eyes open yet with brain cells barely functioning. Although exhausted, I slowly recalled a truth that has helped me to carry on: As I trudged alone through the night hallways, I staggered to a call as old as humankind. That night and every night, mothers and fathers around the world awaken to reassure restless children. That night and every night, grown children arise to calm fitful, aging parents. Those night hours are long and lonely. Our burdens and tired bones are ours alone to bear. There are, however, other people out there who are waking even as we are. There are other people who bear similar burdens—whether it is simply to reassure a child for one night, or to help a dying loved one be at peace, week after week, until the end.

We who rise do so because we choose to do it. It is an intense, physical demand; it is also an honor as ancient as human love. We are part of the circle of families and friends who nurture Life, from its earthly beginning until its earthly conclusion.

## *Prayer of Caregiving*

May the burden of caring
not feel so heavy
as I remember all who have
gone before me
and all who will come after me.

May I know myself to be part of a great dance
that circles and comes round again.
I give thanks for the privilege of caring.
I am home. I am home.

# Laura's Mother

The sweat rolled down my forehead as ubiquitous summer mosquitoes droned around us. My friend Laura paused from the long story she was telling me, pushed back her chair under the old pear tree, and yelled out a warning to one of the kids in the swimming pool. We each took another swallow of lemonade, wiped our brows, and in the momentary quiet, I finally got a chance to ask her something that had been on my mind all afternoon.

Laura is one of the most determined people I know. She has resolved to care for her equally strong-willed yet aging mother. Laura serves as a city councilwoman, is very active in her church, parents two thriving adolescent girls, and heads a school department of many employees. Yet in her heart, there is always room for more.

Laura has taken her mother into her home, wipes up her messes, is cheerful to her mother's eccentric friends, and shuttles her from doctor to doctor in various cities. Despite Laura's usually frenetic pace of teaching, parenting, planning, and serving, she has had to slow down and move at her mother's slower pace. I have seen her mother bark at her, complain and fuss at her. Laura's eyes grow wide, but her lips stay shut.

"Why are you doing this?" I exclaimed. "The demands are just too much! It's above and beyond what you have to do! What are you thinking?"

Laura didn't even pause to think. Her response was un-characteristically short and simple. "She's my mother, Jane. She's my mother."

That was all. And that was everything.

Laura believes she has a role in the cycles of birth and death, of growing and aging. Her role sometimes may be uncom-fortable, inconvenient, and aggravating, but she accepts that as part of the package. Her soul is rooted in the human family.

Life was never comfortable or predictable for Laura—it's even less so now—but she understands. She knows intu-itively that we are all connected, that the life we make for one another is the life we make for ourselves.

# Clubhouse

Working late one afternoon, I forgot that it was my turn to drive my son and another boy to gymnastics. We could still make it, if only I could find Ben. When I drove to the neighbor's house where he was supposed to be playing, he and his buddy were nowhere to be found.

"Maybe they're at the clubhouse!" suggested my daughter Liz.

The clubhouse? What clubhouse? (Mothers are often the last to know about these things.) Liz directed me down a winding gravel road that ended in a vacant lot. "There they are!" she pointed.

I looked out into a partly timbered lot of weeds, grass, and a few scrub trees, lit like gold in the autumn sun. There among the trees I glimpsed two boys bounding like gazelles.

It seems the children have discovered a spot under a fallen tree which, when walled with carpet scraps and roofed with leafy branches, has become a secret place, a "clubhouse" for adventurers, princesses, and pirates. In and around it, they can jump, grow, leap, and fly to new and wonderful places unpopulated by parents and other extraneous adults. Peter Pan would be right at home.

My children tend to make clubhouses wherever they can. The last one that I knew about was on top of our bicycle shed. They placed a ladder against the side and climbed up, hoisted a plastic slide to the ten-foot-high roof, and covered it with a rain tarp. Voila, instant clubhouse. One serious drawback, however, was that our two-year-old climbed up one day and made herself at home when no one was looking. After she was discovered and rescued, and after I finished hyperventilating from anxiety, I called an end to a clubhouse at that location.

Forever undaunted, the children have made a better clubhouse in the vacant lot. And when something happens to that one, they will find another. They naturally seek to create that kind of place people the world over long for, a safe and beautiful haven where their spirits can roam free.

Each of us needs a clubhouse, a place where we can be at home, where we can gather with other dreamers and adventurers. A home, a church, or a bench in the city park can be a clubhouse. The people in a real clubhouse do not ask us to adapt so much as to dream, not of the world as it is, but of the world as it should be.

# *Mardi Gras*

Another Mardi Gras has come and gone. I had big hopes for this one. My children were finally old enough to take to New Orleans for the "Big Time." We were going to get up at the crack of dawn and see the Zulu parade and Rex parade and *all* the truck parades. We were going to catch beads (*long* ones) and cups and lots of cheap plastic trinkets. We were going to get a table at a restaurant on the main avenue so we could eat lavishly all day.

In the days preceding the holiday, I finished my week's work in several long evenings at the phone and the computer so that I could take the time off. My husband and I purchased tickets for a grand ball on the Friday night preceding Mardi Gras, planning to dance all night and start the four-day weekend right.

Fantastic jazz bands played at the ball as we marched and danced with the wild crowd. We laughed with friends old and new. And just around midnight, as the party was reaching fever-pitch, Harry looked at me and said "I feel sick." I felt his head. He was burning with his own raging fever. We went home.

The next few days were not what I had hoped they would be. Feeling cheated and depressed, I cooked, cleaned, and catered to a sick husband and three sick children. "Flu-like virus," the doctor said. "Go to bed and drink plenty of fluids." For some mysterious reason, I was the only one spared.

On Tuesday, Mardi Gras day, I took my son, the only other person finally well enough to get out of the house, and went to a nearby town's Mardi Gras parade for a few hours. I began the day quite sad, feeling robbed of my dream of a grand New Orleans Mardi Gras. Perhaps it was the laughter and kindness of friends standing along the parade route. Perhaps it was the sunlight warming my face. Perhaps it was the smile on my young son's face. At one decisive moment, I looked up into the eyes of a grinning lady who threw me a long string of beads from the back of a pickup truck and realized that I had finally given up my desire to be in New Orleans.

I had almost lost Mardi Gras to an ancient affliction more insidious than any virus. The Buddhists call it attachment. The Puritans called it greed. I needed to let go of unattainable hopes before my here-and-now could be joyful. How hard it was! How hard it is, every day! A desire for a larger house masks the reality that the present one is warm and comfortable. A desire for more personal free time masks the reality of meaningful work and a loving family.

Mardi Gras came this year, pick-up trucks and all, tossing me a valuable lesson more precious than any plastic pearls. It happened when I let go of my desires and attachments to an unattainable goal and simply began to enjoy the moment. Thank you, pick-up trucks. Thank you, family, friends, and sunlight. Thank you, world.

## Prayer of Awareness

Spirit of many names,
and beyond all names,
may I rest in this moment
and open my eyes to see

*20*   how every tree branch,
every speck of dust on the sidewalk,
every glance of a stranger,
points beyond itself
to you:

the emptiness, the fullness,
the joy, the energy,
the beginning and ending
of all.

Amen.

It was one of those rush-rush days: off to lunch with a church newcomer, to the store for a book for a sermon, to the post office to pick up some packages, to another church member's home for a meeting. Each place I stopped demanded a new attitude and emotion from me. I accomplished each task in turn, then jumped back into the car to rush rush—change car gears, change mental gears. Drive the speed limit (or more) to get here, get there, and then back to my office for an afternoon appointment. Rush rush—thinking, as I drove, not of where I was, but of where I was going next.

And then . . . Wham! I was startled by an unexpected vision. Looming from a drainage ditch alongside a highway access road was the tallest, whitest egret I have ever seen. Unperturbed by the booming traffic only a few feet away, the egret towered above the grass, its unearthly long neck extended far in front of its body. It stood unmoving, in a stance of extreme concentration, pointing its head at prey hidden in a small clump of grass that had eluded the mowers.

What beauty and grace! Still framed in my rear-view mirror, slowly shrinking from view, the egret stood transfixed despite the speediness of everything around it.

As far as I know, the bird is still standing there, pointing for anyone who will notice. When I think of it today, I give thanks. It reminded me that although rush rush sometimes gets me where I need to go, it doesn't take me into the heart of Life.

# *Breathing*

As part of our "check-out" dive at the beginning of a scuba diving vacation, I was demonstrating basic skills to my divemaster. He knelt on the bottom of the bay a few feet away from me, serene and unflappable, watching me struggle. I had removed my mask, a basic exercise, and now I had to put it back on and fill it with air blown through my nose. Trouble was, no amount of blowing would fill it. Finally, after watching me struggle for a good minute with sea water seeping into my nose and my eyes stinging terribly, the divemaster leaned over and held the top of my mask to my face. It immediately filled with air. Instead of holding the top, I had been holding the bottom of my mask to my face, which let the air escape out the top—an embarrassing novice's mistake!

But I didn't forget to keep breathing!

When something goes wrong underwater, the first thing you're taught is to regain mental control by breathing slowly and regularly. And when there is no air to breathe, you must have the self-discipline to act carefully, without fear, to find an air source. How you breathe underwater not only determines the quality of your experience, but it also sustains your life. Breathe too deeply and you may run out of air if you don't pay attention. Breathe too quickly and shallowly and you'll hyperventilate, pass out, and drown. Hold your breath when you are ascending and your lungs will explode.

After completing all the other check-out skills, the divemaster indicated that I was to remove my mask and to replace it again. This was the last thing I wanted to do. But I did it, and I did it right this time. The only way I was able to maintain control and finish the exercise was to keep breathing, slow and steady.

Breathing. Buddhist masters and divemasters agree on this point: awareness of the moment, even our very lives, depends on awareness of our breath.

# Time

I don't seem to have enough time today. The clocks have portioned it out and have given me only twenty-four hours—not nearly the amount I need to get everything done. I try to fit all my appointments and necessary tasks neatly into the little squares on my calendar and the cubicles in my heart, but there isn't enough room.

If I had only two more hours, 120 more minutes, 7,200 more seconds, to my day, perhaps I would get it all done. Or maybe I need three hours more. Would that be enough? Or would eternity be enough to satisfy me?

I watch the clock. It is moving faster than I ever can. I try to match my speed to that of the hands moving too rapidly around the clock face. At this rate I have barely enough time to breathe, let alone accomplish anything.

Yet a small voice deep inside me tries to be heard: "You have it all wrong!" Then I remember a man I once knew who collected clocks. On the outside he was a proper gentleman and a well-known citizen of his city. But within him dwelt a denizen of the realm of Father Time. My friend's large, well-appointed study was filled with dozens of clocks of every size and description. He didn't wind up *all* of them, yet when I sat in that room, there were enough tic tocs to fill every corner of my consciousness with the cricketing of what seemed a thousand wound toys. After a few minutes of listening, the sound flowed into every bit of space and time until I was no longer conscious of the noise or the passage of time.

If all the clocks in the world were gathered in one large room, perhaps we could understand that there is no past and no future by the clock. We live in no other time but the present. Understanding this is as close as we can get to understanding eternal life.

Perhaps, after all, I have enough time . . .

# The Lemonade Issue

Women were stretched out around my coffee table, reaching for tea and potato chips. They had gathered because I needed cheap help to deal with a tough life situation. "What do you do," I wondered aloud, "when something really rotten has happened and you keep trying to see some good come of it?"

"Lemons into lemonade, you mean?" muttered one friend. "That has been my task my whole life. I'm ready for another!"

"The lemonade issue, huh?" another friend sputtered. "I've been focused on that for years! And I'm wiped out. I'm trying so hard to not dwell on the problems, but to see the positive possibilities instead. And I'm tired of it. I'm all out of psychic energy. It's like work that I can't seem to really do right."

"Maybe we've gotta stop forcing it," someone else suggested. "It never seems to happen if I force it. But sometimes, when I look back, if I've tried to stay creative, then maybe something comes of it."

"Hey, don't you know about Bela Bartok and the soldiers?" said a musician friend. The faces around the coffee table were uniformly blank. "Bela Bartok—you know, the great composer—was living in Budapest immediately after World War II. The city was occupied by Romanian soldiers and some of them occupied his apartment. Bartok got to know them by asking them to sing Romanian folk songs, which he then wrote down and orchestrated. This collection became known as one of his greatest works. The songs are now played by major symphonies around the world. Is this what you mean by lemons to lemonade?"

Few of us around that coffee table—or around any coffee table in my neighborhood—may have the genius of Bela Bartok, but my friend certainly had a point. Instead of trying to force a message from our pain, perhaps a little more Bartok-ism would help: Pick up the materials we like to use to express ourselves and let the juices flow. Creativity is transforming, whether with paints, words, musical notes, or lemons!

If we can find a song or a story, or even a great new recipe, we may be able to paint, cook, write, or conjure up our own gate to healing.

## Italian Dressing

Sometimes I believe I finally have my act together. I've had enough sleep the night before, my clothes look good, it's not a bad hair day, and I feel like I have just the right mix of witty-alert-empathetic to get me through the day on a roll. Then the Trickster steps in and reminds me that it's never so simple, that joy usually springs not from orderliness but from its opposite.

It happened at a local clergy Christmas luncheon. The meal was lovely. The ambiance, in the private dining room of a local hospital, was gracious. The company was magnificent. Twenty or so brother and sister clergy from my area were there and I was having a wonderful time conversing and telling stories with fellow pastors at my table and throughout the room.

A presenter stood up to tell us of his institution's good work. I sat back in my chair and nodded knowingly, listening carefully to his story. Nevertheless, I was thirsty and gracefully stood up, walked to the beverage table in the back of the room and carefully poured myself a glass of iced tea. I picked up a handy plastic packet of lemon juice. When I returned to the table, I stirred it all up and took a large swallow.

Gasp! Something was terribly wrong with my iced tea! My eyes watered and turned red as I choked loudly into my napkin. I imagined my colleagues casting me side-long glances while trying to keep their attention focused on the speaker. I took a good look at my glass. Chunks of some-thing too large to be lemon were swimming around in my iced tea. I picked up the lemon juice packet, now lying empty on my plate. It was Italian Dressing.

The Trickster had struck, just when I needed him most.

Many Native American stories tell of a Trickster—often Coyote—who steps in to stir things up and remind us not to take ourselves too seriously. I suppose I should be lucky that it was just Italian dressing. I clearly remember looking at and reading the lemon juice packet before adding its contents to my tea. The Trickster must have arranged for me to read "lemon" instead of "Italian." Something deep inside knew I needed a little shaking up.

Just when pretense begins to feel like reality, it helps to be reminded that life is wild, crazy, and gleeful. The God-spirit, the creative urge, the energy of all earth and all life can be found in sunrises, in rainbows, in unexpected sticky kisses, in wide-eyed sputtering, and in all sorts of surprises.

Children are good at reminding us of that.

So is Italian dressing.

# Cat People and Dog People

There are two kinds of people in this world: cat people and dog people. I tried to be a cat person not long ago. My family even bought a house that came equipped with its own cat, a pretty white kitten that had been abandoned by its previous owners. We immediately adopted her and tried to love her. But cats, as Snowflake immediately notified me, allow themselves to be loved only on their own terms and at their discretion.

Cat people, Snowflake reminded me, must have a strong sense of who they are, and be able to nurture themselves. They must be able to appreciate radical individualism. Cat people (forgive me if I slander) must also find some perverse satisfaction in loving someone who will never love them back.

It must be clear by now that I am, and always will be, a dog person. After putting up with our family for a year, Snowflake departed our neighborhood. Her leaving made room in our family psyche for what the children and I had long desired: a dog.

The newest addition to our family is a beautiful English springer spaniel named Hanna. She loves her people pathetically, licking my toes if I will let her. She begs to be around us, and is miserable when we are gone for any length of time. She desperately needs us, and we dog people, who so want to be needed, eat it up.

As a solid dog person since age four, I can say honestly that dog people are deeply interdependent. We need to be needed; we want to be slobbered over! We love cavorting like children and whispering sweet nothings to adoring eyes. There is nothing quite like the complete devotion of a dog, and we love it.

This world needs both kinds of people: cat people, who are able to work independently and quietly, content to know they are making a solid difference in the PTA, church, or synagogue, and dog people, who make lots of noise, organize ball games, frolic with children, and tell everyone how wonderful they are.

However, the next time a stray cat comes to my house, I won't try to change my basic nature. I'm calling a cat person to come take it off my hands.

# *Hanna*

I have a big springer spaniel named Hanna who is the joy and bane of my life. I grew up with English springer spaniels and once Harry and I had children, I naturally wanted to fill out the family with a dog. We got Hanna on the first night of Hanukkah a few years ago. She is a very ecumenical dog: her full name is "Hanukkah Star." I got Christmas Eve in there, too.

I have learned a lot from Hanna. I no longer expect her to fit any stereotype or model. She hasn't learned, despite all my best dog-training methods, not to jump onto the sofa when she wants to see out the front window. She still doesn't understand that the huge Husky across the street— her neighbor all her life—could stop her cold in her tracks forever if he wanted to. She doesn't realize that it is in her best interest to stop barking and chasing him. Little things like that. You would think she'd learn.

On the other hand, you would think I'd learn. Hanna has a mind of her own, interests of her own, passions of her own. She doesn't live for my benefit; she lives to live, to enjoy life, to chase squirrels and wrestle with children and doze in the sun.

We have a fairly symbiotic relationship: I feed her and she looks up at me with big brown eyes and adores me, even when I'm at my most cranky. I suppose she has taught me much more than I have given her. She has shown me that animals—and through her, all of nature—are not here for my benefit or pleasure. As Emerson once wrote, "Beauty is its own excuse for being." The trees, the squirrels, and the air we both breathe are here for us to participate in and to appreciate, not to own or master.

I live with Hanna. I am responsible for her well-being. Yet, she is not mine. We are co-inhabitants of a house on 15th Avenue . . . and of planet Earth.

# Monarchs and Mystery

I am frequently astonished by monarch butterflies. Delicate beyond belief, they fly thousands of miles each year from all parts of the continent to settle in the forests of South America. To my delight, their migratory route takes them along a bridge near my home.

A few days ago, I was driving on this bridge during their annual display of fragility and strength. As my car whipped by at over sixty miles per hour, the tiny creatures were tossed haphazardly by the winds, yet I knew there was a continual southward purpose to their struggle.

Much as I admired these fragile butterflies, I could not avoid hitting several of them. While orange wings smashed into my windshield, I remembered a chilling science fiction story I had read as a child. A man of the near future travels back in time to the age of the dinosaurs to sightsee in that era. Despite the tour guide's warnings, he leaves the path in his excitement and while in the underbrush steps on and kills one tiny, fragile butterfly. When he returns to his own time, the world is horribly different: people are much crueler and an international fascist government now rules. The death of one butterfly in the distant past has changed all of world history.

As I travel the many miles of the bridge during the annual monarch butterfly migration, I wonder if I am wreaking any changes in the world to come. What effect do my words and deeds—both on the bridge and off—make in the environment and in the human world? Surely they do make a difference. Our kindness affects lives we will never see. Our cruelty casts ripples that may drown strangers.

Whether smashing butterflies or helping a friend, our actions will echo through history. We will not always know the ramifications of our deeds, but they are there. We are surely connected, one to another, and each of us to the greater world of monarchs and mystery.

# What the Chicken Taught

I dislike harming any animal, even ants, so killing our chicken was not how I had planned to spend the morning.

This was a rather special chicken, as chickens go. Beloved friends gave us four chickens a while back, but some varmint came out of the woods and got three of them right away. This chicken, however, had the wit to survive. She also had a grain of defiance. She wouldn't stay caged in a safe pen. Every morning, she flew over the pen fence and spent the day pecking around the yard. I liked her, I liked her defiance, and she seemed to like us. She often came up the eight steps onto our back porch and poked around, leaving her droppings (which I didn't like) as reminders of her chickenness. Some evenings we were able to entice her back inside the pen, but other times, including last night, she continued to roam. Her freedom was her downfall.

We found her by the back porch steps this morning. She looked at us calmly, eyes blinking. The entire back part of her body had been ripped open by some creature with claws. Harry and I knew what we had to do. We loaded the kids into the car and I backed the car out of the yard while he took the shovel blade to the chicken. After Harry got in the car and drove away to run errands, I walked back alone to perform the burial and found her still alive, breathing and looking at me. I did what I had to do, cursing, crying, and praying simultaneously.

"Please die, chicken. Please die!"

"I'm sorry, chicken. I'm sorry!"

Chickens are hard to kill. I am basically a city kid and did not know this, remembering only the story of my great-grandmother who could wring a chicken's neck with one twist. My chicken didn't die that way. After it was all over, I buried her at the edge of the woods.

Today I am shaken and sad. How far I have come from my great-grandmother's time of relying on home gardens and home chickens for food and survival. How far I have come from being part of the everyday cycles of life and death. I feel as if I have forgotten some basic knowledge.

Life is more simple and fleeting than I like to pretend. I am feeling very animal now, flesh and blood, breath and fur, aware of the transience of my animal body. That chicken clung to life fiercely. But in the end, she was delicate bones that broke. My bones feel more frail today. My breath feels quicker. I am awed by how fragile and fleeting and extremely precious life is.

Thank you, chicken. Thank you.

# Oklahoma City

When the evening news came on Wednesday, April 19, 1995, the concrete and steel Murrah Building in Oklahoma City tumbled out of the TV screen and onto my heart.

The people could have been my people—my children, my husband, my friends whom I love so much.

To my shame, I thought immediately of Middle Eastern terrorists. This was Middle America, Oklahoma City, where I had lived for a time during college, where I have visited many times, and where I feel at home with the rhythms, the drawl, the friendly people—*my* people. Someone was attacking us. It was time to circle the wagons, to "draw a circle to leave him out, a heretic, a rebel, a thing to flout. . . ."

Then further news came. It was no foreigner. The suspect was a blue-eyed, all-American guy with a crew cut, a man with a young child, respectable high school attendance, and military service.

I do not believe in original sin. Never have. Never will. Yet, neither are we the "saved" people. Within each of us lies the capability to do good and to do evil. We must choose, every day. Likewise, our laws and our government are not the best on earth nor the worst. America does not contain a fatal flaw that must be destroyed or corrected, but it has long been the breeding ground for many possibilities.

It would have been easier to understand the bombing if the bomber had been someone I could view as an outsider intent on destroying America. Instead, the bombing demanded that I begin, with my country and my people, an intense period of self-examination. Who are we, really? There was no possibility of circling the wagons because we were already inside the circle where a deadly hatred had fostered.

I mourn for the children, the men, and the women whose deaths were the result of bitter hate among us. We must find an antidote. The clues for one can be found in the actions of thousands of people who gave and helped over the weeks, months, and years following the bombing. They bring me hope.

## Prayer for Healing

Torn and confused,
lonely and enraged,
I greet the new day with suspicion.

Spirit of Life,
show me the gate to healing.
May I find in my hands the tools
to craft a way through the pain.

When even those tools fail me,
may other hands reach out.
Let me welcome them,
and know them as your hands,
gently holding me,
keeping me from collapse,
shaping me and molding new strength
until I am ready to try again.

Amen.

# *Conscience*

It's not easy having a conscience. We have a lot to lose, and sometimes we have to be ready to lose it.

A good friend almost lost a great deal while trying to live her conscience. She had been searching for her dream house, spending weekends and vacations in another state where she hoped to retire. Finally, she found the perfect place. It was love at first sight, the price was unbelievably low, and, miracle of miracles, her offer was immediately accepted.

My friend did lots of research to prepare for the "closing." She discovered the house title carried a "restrictive covenant," which stated the house could not be resold to anyone of a racial minority. This restriction was against the law, but it was still in the title. My friend told her lawyer to make sure this statement was not in the title at closing time. He assured her it would be taken care of.

Closing day came around. She took two days off work to travel to the closing appointment. Sellers, realtors, lawyers, and my friend all pulled up around the table and she was handed the papers to sign. "It's all as we've agreed," her lawyer assured her. But my friend carefully read everything one last time. There it was: house not to be resold to member of a racial minority.

"I'm sorry. I can't sign this!" she declared.

"What??!!" was the reaction.

"I'm sorry. I told you all I can't sign with this restrictive covenant."

"Well," the lawyers said, "it's all drawn up. We can't change it now."

"Well, I can't sign it." My friend stood up to leave and walked for the door.

There was no small amount of consternation and scurrying about. The papers were changed, the restrictive covenant was removed, and she bought the house that day.

Later, her lawyer said, "You know, you were right. My daughter is in law school. I'm going to tell her what you did. She's going to think that was great!"

That woman was my mother. And her daughter thinks she's pretty great, too.

The ripples of our actions, when we live as our conscience dictates, wash upon distant shores, and reshape our world, one heart, one neighborhood, one town, one generation at a time.

Shake me awake
when I cover my ears,
when I deny your call,
and try to justify my actions with
greed called practicality,
hunger called need,
desire called just desserts.

Flood my hearing with
the music of love
that pounds through my veins.

May my craving cease
and my sensitivity heighten
that each moment each day
my ears and heart are open
to you.

Amen.

# Front Page News

I like to begin my morning with a cup of Earl Grey tea and the morning paper. I start with the comics and Ann Landers, then once I'm fortified (and the caffeine has begun to kick in), I'm ready to face The Front Page. On a recent morning, the big story was about eighty-some-odd nations signing an international treaty banning land mines—but United States leaders refused to sign.

A US representative explained that the US government did not want to forego the use of land mines along the North Korea–South Korea border, and added, "we believe that land mines can be made which are efficient and safe."

Safe land mines? Are land mines "safe" if they *just* blow away the lives and limbs of young soldiers? Are they "unsafe" if they blow away the lives and limbs of young and old alike, after a war has ended?

When did bombs become "smart" and land mines become "safe"? My second cup of Earl Grey tea slowly lost its heat as I quickly blew my cool, thinking of the ways I have heard perfectly decent words manipulated for the purpose of converting kind hearts to destructive purposes.

Our language can be used for good, for connection, for building relationships, and for binding the broken. And it can also destroy, mutilate, and, worst of all, *seduce*.

That morning, the comics made more sense than the front page news. And I said a prayer for all whose lives would be destroyed by land mines, "safe" and otherwise.

## Perfect Christmas Gift

Each Christmas, despite my past experiences, I strive for and expect perfection. I sally forth in quest of the perfect Christmas gift, the perfect Christmas experience, and the perfect Christmas worship service.

Each year it's the same. I don't seem to learn. Three years ago, I bought my husband the perfect gift, an exquisite, Swiss Army knife from a notable catalog company. Harry used it continually for three months until the front and back of the case fell off and it became impossible to open.

Two years ago, Santa brought my son the perfect surprise, an electric train set. I was extremely proud of the set and helped Santa set it up late Christmas Eve. The next morning, the engine wouldn't stay on the tracks and the little pieces kept breaking. It was a clunker.

A year ago, departing from our congregation's traditional, beloved Candles and Carols service, I wrote (I thought) a perfect Christmas Eve service, telling the Christmas story with the poetry of W. H. Auden. It was thick and dense. The children in attendance were completely lost and even my family didn't "get it."

I continue to be disappointed with my strivings at Christmas time, yet isn't that what Christmas is all about? The Christmas myth is a story about something special happening in the midst of imperfection. After all, Jesus was—

shall we say—an unplanned pregnancy. His mother gave birth while far from home. Joseph and Mary were poor and their child was born in a stable. The locals weren't exactly thrilled with the baby. His parents had to flee to Egypt to save his life.

It helps me to remember these things about the Christmas story. I feel at home in this part of the myth, for my failings and disappointments continue unabated through December, and family squabbles invariably increase at this time of year. Yet, in all these imperfections, the true meaning of Christmas can be found.

Christmas isn't about perfection. It is about love in the thick of our daily lives: human love, family love, being glad we have one another. For us fussbudgets the angels sing. Glory, hallelujah! Now please pick up your socks.

## Howard Hughes Syndrome

Christmas morning has its own ritual in our household. The children have been instructed to sleep until *at least* 6:00 a.m. Grudgingly they set their alarms, and at 6:01 begin yelling from their bedrooms.

Harry and I stagger forth, exhausted from helping Santa put together puppet theaters and such until the wee hours of the morning. We switch on the Christmas tree lights, take the youngest child to the bathroom so that she can participate in the "moment," and then, with three panting children, storm into the living room to feast our eyes on the bounty. Packages and presents that miraculously appeared overnight are heaped around the tree in glorious profusion. The children yell with glee and plunge in.

Wild exclamations, giggling, and ripping of paper continue for an hour or so. When the last package is ripped open and the last stocking emptied, the children look up amazed, "Is that all?"

Each year without fail they are hit by an ancient truth they try hard to forget: no train or doll or CD player or any other item that can be wrapped and unwrapped will really bring them happiness. They seem startled each year at this discovery. Harry and I, having fallen once again into the seasonal commercial trap and hoping (again each year) that we can somehow purchase a happy childhood for our children, hear the question and wake up, too. "Is that all?"

My friend Tsultrim calls this the Howard Hughes syndrome. Hughes kept everything he could for himself, craving some kind of happiness that forever eluded him. He also wore gloves because he believed he would get dirty if he touched another person.

Each Christmas morning I become aware that we each have a little Howard in us. We think if we could just get rich enough and clean enough, if we could just get enough toys or clothes or books, we finally will be happy.

An antidote to the Howard Hughes syndrome is gratitude. My family seems to realize this intuitively and we begin to give thanks at the breakfast table. First, the expected and rote: thank you for the candlestick, thank you for the book. Slowly we wait for the spirit that lit the first Christmas lights to illuminate our hearts. Only then can we move into real gratitude: I am thankful we are healthy. I am thankful we have this food. I am thankful for my family, and that we can be together. We take off our Howard Hughes gloves and we hold hands.

By Christmas afternoon, we realize that the real gifts of Christmas are the laughter we hear in each other's voices, the wind in our hair as we race on the lawn, the love we have to share as we read new books together. If we are truly lucky, this realization will stay with us long after the presents are broken or worn out . . . at very best, until holiday catalogs start arriving the following autumn.

Someday, I pray, we will remember all this at 6:00 a.m. on Christmas morning.

The year my brother died, my family tried to pretend our sorrow wasn't real and we kept to all our regular Christmas traditions. Although we were crazed with grief, we tried to fake it and were all miserable.

Later, when my father died, my mother decided we should take a trip for the holidays instead of staying home and being overwhelmed by memories.

"But it won't be like Christmas!" my teenaged brother protested.

"It can never be like it has been before," replied my mother.

Concord, Massachusetts, was our destination. We checked into historic Concord Inn on the public square and spent three days exploring the wintry village. We walked across the bridge from which the shot was fired that was heard 'round the world. We discovered paths in the snow around Emerson's house and the Alcott house. We slid across the ice on Walden Pond. It was a wonderful adventure, but at the same time we were all unhappy. We spent Christmas Eve in the inn's pub, and I was not alone in crying myself to sleep that night.

Early on Christmas morning, my mother and I rose at dawn. Leaving my brother asleep, we slipped out for a walk. It was a frosty but clear morning. A fresh layer of snow had utterly muffled the town. For deep, unspoken reasons, we headed up a hill to the old cemetery where many great authors and American leaders are buried. We were looking for the grave of poet Henry David Thoreau. The dirt walkway up the hill was quite steep and coated in thick ice. We pulled ourselves up hand-over-hand using the iron handrail. As we reached the top, the steam of our breaths appeared to be the only lively warmth in the chilly, pink dawn. After a search, we spied Thoreau's grave, a large tombstone cresting out of a snowdrift. And there, to our astonishment and joy, lay a single red rose. No one else was in sight, but some lone soul had made his or her pilgrimage in the first light of Christmas Day to salute that free spirit.

My family no longer "does Christmas" as we once did. Each year is now unique, and I like it that way. I have fewer expectations of Christmas and enjoy myself more. I live less in the past and try to appreciate my life here and now.

Let go of what Christmas "should be" and try to live it in your own way. You may find joy where you least expect it: a red rose in the snow.

# *Prayer in Action*

A number of years ago, my brother lay dying in the hospital. He spent days in the intensive care unit while members of my family, including my mother, sat for many long hours on chairs in the hallway outside his room. Among the visitors who came to share the vigil was a member of our church.

"How are you doing?" the friend asked.

My mother was too exhausted to tell anything but the truth. "I'm tired," she said. "I'm very, very tired. I'm too tired to even pray any more."

"But don't you see," her friend replied, "your very presence here is a prayer."

There are times when all words fail us, all forms seem hollow, and no one out there or inside seems to be listening. At those times, our presence, just our presence, is prayer. Our bodies, our actions, become our prayer, our connection to God, whatever God may be.

## Prayer for Faith

So often words fail us
And we do not know to whom or what to pray.

We ask for legs that can walk for peace,
Arms that can work for justice,
Voices that can speak with love,
Hands that can soothe a feverish brow.

By our actions and voices
May our prayers be sent.

Shalom. Salaam. Om. Amen.

# *Throwing Pots*

In my otherwise tidy life, I love the muddiness of throwing pots. I love making something from nothing. I can take a new pot home, stick a flower in it, and say: I made that. It is real. But most of all, I love the grace of throwing pots. No matter what my plans for a particular hunk of clay, it invariably becomes something else. Either I can be disappointed or I can rejoice in its new incarnation. In my daily life, I like to plan, to figure, to organize in order to work toward the very best outcome. Pots don't do that. They evolve. In the end, they are what they are, and all my best plans are as dust—or mud.

Today I set a new bowl on my counter and I remember what the clay has taught me. I had specific plans for this bowl and carefully shaped it to be tall and narrow, to be a vase for my garden zinnias. In the shaping, however, the sides of the bowl took a dive south and I now have a wide shallow container, just right for fruit. It's not what I expected, but with the white and blue glazes it is beautiful anyway.

I have big plans for my weekend. I have big plans for my life. Yet the bowl laughs at me. The clay laughs at me. Don't take your plans too seriously, they say, for life will no doubt hand you something altogether surprising. Although it may be a bit lumpy, it will have its own special beauty.

## Wanting a Bike

The boy wants a bicycle. Not just any bike will do. He wants a special "trick-bike," one with bells and whistles and lots of pizzazz, one that will leap tall buildings with a single bound. Or so it seems to his mom. She is discouraged. The boy already has a bike, a good one, a solid ride-it-to-school-and-the-library bike. She has tried talking to him: "In my day, kids were happy with . . ." "One bike is enough!" "We just don't have the money right now!"

The boy is sure, however, that *this* bike will be the fulfillment of his dreams, the answer to his prayers, the one thing in the world that will bring him true happiness.

The mom has private dreams of her own. If she could just get the recognition that she has so long hoped for at her job . . . if she could just take that special trip to Mexico she has wanted for years . . . if she could just lose ten pounds . . . surely *then* she would be happy. It's so easy to believe that some *thing* will make them happy (or, in the case of the ten pounds, lack of some thing).

No, no, say the wise ones. It's not the things, the stuff, the bikes, and banners. It's your awareness of where you are. It's being awake. "Open your eyes," they say. "Look," they say. "Get a life!" they say.

Deep inside themselves, the boy and mom know this. But it is easier to buy a bike or even to diet than it is to live with eyes open. It is easier to rest their hopes on almost anything than it is to forego desire and find their ecstasy in the moment they are now alive.

# *Penguins*

One night not long ago, a little girl was being tucked into bed by her mother. The mom, although tired and cranky, still remembered to go through the ritual of tuck, listen, cuddle, and kiss. She was trying to do it quickly this evening, for dishes, laundry, and other work still stood between her and her own collapse into bed. Thus, the mother was only half-aware when her daughter began speaking.

"My birds come to me in my sleep, Mom."

"What?" asked the mother, startled.

"My birds, you know, the penguins." The child sat up and pointed to a zoo poster over her bed on which appeared a long line of penguins sitting on an ice floe, the bright pink and purple winter sky behind them.

"Your birds come to you in your sleep?" By now the mother was fully awake and listening intently.

"Yes. That one, and that one, and that one, and especially the baby one." She chose three black and white individuals, recognizing something special in their appearance, and concluded with the furry gray immature penguin at the end of the line.

"What do they do, when they come to you in your sleep?" The woman watched her daughter curiously.

"They bring me good gifts." She smiled shyly and lay back down. "They take me outside to show me the sky. And sometimes they fold their wings over my eyes like this to bring me beautiful thoughts." She folded her arms over her face. Her demonstration done, the child turned over. "Good night, Mom."

"I love you. Good night, sweetheart." The mother concluded the ritual with a kiss, stood up, and left the room amazed and delighted.

Months earlier, during a trip to the local zoo, she had given the child a choice of several posters. All but one showed a bright, colorful menagerie of various animals in beautiful environments. The girl had refused the more colorful posters and chose the line-up of penguins. How dull, the mother had thought. How unimaginative, compared to white tigers, alligators, or toucans. She had reluctantly agreed to the girl's choice, concluding that she must not have encouraged her daughter to be daring or adventurous if the girl chose a bunch of black and white penguins over a jungle scene or a florescent coral reef.

Later that evening, the mother took a deep breath as she did the dishes. She realized she was the one who lacked imagination. Focused on her own ideas about color and design, she had missed the beauty and magic in the penguin poster and in her own daughter's mind. The penguins had brought her a "good gift." It was a reminder to be humble in the presence of the mystery of each human heart.

# *Waiting in Right Field*

The Olympics roll around every two years. The event is over-hyped, over-reported, and blatantly nationalistic. But still, ya gotta love it! Catching the spirit every two years, I wonder anew: Who will be the great champions of our time? Who will be swifter, higher, stronger?

In the smaller universe of my town, each season brings youth sports tournaments that elicit considerable passion from the participants and their parents. My favorites are the summer baseball tournaments. Lots of neighborhood children participate. These kids are truly dedicated athletes. They get out on the hot field, hour after hour, to pitch, throw, run, bat, and (more often) simply stand and watch and wait for one more opportunity to do their best. Finally, in the season's-end tournaments, only one team in each age group is declared the winner.

Many of us old-timers have memories of participating in team sports. When I watch children on the field each summer, I remember the Eisenhower Honeybees. The coaches, to their credit (and probably embarrassment) let our motley crew of fifth-grade Oklahoma girls from Eisenhower Elementary name our own team. We even chose our own team colors: pink and white. Clearly not a bunch of toughs. I spent my softball career with the Honeybees way out in right field and, whenever they let me bat, always striking out. I remember seeing lots of interesting bugs and clouds out there in right field—Tulsa's version of *Peanuts'* Lucy.

My heart goes out to the child at bat who swings and swings and swings again, the one who sits eagerly on the bench, anxiously waiting to hear his or her name called as the coach yells out assignments, then stumbles out to right field once again (or even more likely, remains on the bench). Each of us has been there, in one way or another. Even the star pitcher of the championship team is, at other times, the class stooge in algebra, or fighting what feels like terminal acne. We can only pray that surviving such travails will make us softer, not harder; kinder, not crueler.

Perhaps I love the Olympics because I have been there, too. When I look past the hype, the commercialization, and the blather, something about the Olympics feels as familiar as the Honeybees' right field. Most of the Olympic athletes won't win a thing; they just hope for a chance to do their best. As I watch them, pushing and struggling, I'm back in my own home town, standing in the new grass, praying that the ball will come to me and that, once, just once, I will catch it.

I once thought that I was going to die. Not just in-the-future-it-happens-to-all-of-us-because-we-are-mortal die, but *die now*. I didn't die, but I learned a little humility along the way.

My husband and I were coming home from our first adults-only vacation in years. As I was pregnant with our third child, we also knew that it would be our last adults-only vacation for a long time to come.

Approaching home, the plane flew through terrible storms. I have flown many times in bad weather, but this was different. Thunder roared around us without ceasing; the plane tossed and fell like a bird in a tornado. As the storm mounted in intensity, I began to focus not on what might go right, but on what might go wrong. I remembered how unorganized people and procedures had been earlier at the airport. I remembered the youth of the pilots.

Then I remembered one more thing: An old woman had read my palm at a wedding years ago and had remarked purposefully that I would have two children and would die young. My memory of this very suspicious, unscientific statement, thrown into the brew of my observations about the airline and the storm, and mixed with a good dose of pregnancy hormones resulted in the obvious conclusion: We were all going to die.

I prepared myself for the end. First, I told Harry I loved him. (He looked at me kindly and patted me on the knee.) Next, I thought of how my children would respond to the news of our deaths. I cried as I thought of their grief and pain. I knew that they would be raised by loving family members. They would be all right.

Then, I turned to the serious business at hand. I focused my concentration on the light that I thought was sure to come. Would there be a long, dark tunnel with a blazing sun at the end? Would there be a rebirth somehow? I did not know the answers. All that seemed important was to feel peaceful, calm, and loving. That attitude, felt deep in my heart, seemed to be the most appropriate way to meet death.

And then the plane broke through the clouds. It had stopped twisting and churning and headed straight for the runway. As we touched down, a loud cheer erupted throughout the aircraft. We were down. We were safe. We were not going to die at this time. I broke into sobs, shaking with the intensity of my experience.

A few minutes later, as we were preparing to get off the plane, I found myself perturbed with the clumsy people ahead of me. I complained testily to Harry. He looked at me quietly. "You don't sound like someone who just thought she was going to die." Then I remembered the attitude of love for everyone and everything that I felt was the way to meet death. Surely it is the best way to meet life, too. If I could maintain that focus, I would be ready for every moment, whatever that moment would bring. I can't do it all the time—it's difficult to do it even some of the time—but it's worth a try.

# Damp and Oozy

It's another rainy morning at the doctor's office. I sit, overstimulated and waiting, my head full of the crud that brought me here. My young children cough enticingly into my face ("Here, Mom, if you don't have enough germs already, you can share mine!").

I do not like to wait. I prefer to be going, running, driving, typing, *accomplishing*, for Pete's sake. Yet here I sit, waiting.

I assume there is a lesson somewhere in my visits here. You know the lesson. You could write it yourself: "Be here now. Live for the moment. Relax." I'm certainly much better at preaching it than living it. Right now, as I sneeze, blow, and wipe runny noses, I would rather not be here at all, lesson or no lesson.

Jesus is reported to have said, "Split the wood and you shall find me. Lift the stone and there I am." In other words, the holiness of life can be found in damp, moist, oozy, natural places, too. Well, my family has damp, moist, and oozy down pretty well. The holy, huh? Right here, huh?

Perhaps this is a test. It's much easier to see the holy revealed in the stars at night, or in the glory of a great choral "Hallelujah!" But here, in a moment filled with waiting-room noise, diaper bags, and sinus headaches, if I can find it, it oughta be easy the rest of the time.

This list includes all meditation manuals since the merger in 1961. For information about meditations prior to 1961, contact Skinner House Books, 25 Beacon Street, Boston, MA 02108.

1998    *Glory Hallelujah! Now Please Pick Up Your Socks*
            Jane Ellen Mauldin
        *Evening Tide*  Elizabeth Tarbox
1997    *A Temporary State of Grace*  David S. Blanchard
        *Green Mountain Spring and Other Leaps of Faith*
            Gary A. Kowalski
1996    *Taking Pictures of God*  Bruce T. Marshall
        *Blessing the Bread*  Lynn Unger
1995    *In the Holy Quiet of This Hour*  Richard S. Gilbert
1994    *In the Simple Morning Light*  Barbara Rohde
1993    *Life Tides*  Elizabeth Tarbox
        *The Gospel of Universalism*  Tom Owen-Towle
1992    *Noisy Stones*  Robert R. Walsh
1991    *Been in the Storm So Long*  Mark Morrison-Reed
            and Jacqui James, Editors
1990    *Into the Wilderness*  Sara Moores Campbell
1989    *A Small Heaven*  Jane Ranney Rzepka
1988    *The Numbering of Our Days*
            Anthony Friess Perrino
1987    *Exaltation*  David B. Parke, Editor